The Lies That Bind

Understanding and overcoming
the spiritual opposition set against you.

by
Dave MacLean

For all the valiant, courageous, overwhelmed, ordinary Jesus-followers who everyday keep pressing on through an unseen opposition to appropriate all our Lord has accomplished for us, and for others through us.

Well done.

Soli Deo Gloria

TABLE OF CONTENTS

ACKNOWLEDGEMENTS

There are a select few I want to thank for this extraordinary journey I have been on for the last decade. To my Band of Brothers – Stephen, Ben and Brad – thank you for choosing to stay in the adventure amidst the beauty and the brokenness.

To my valiant sons David and Benjamin who help adjust my "Viz" on a regular basis.

To Gregg Cochrane whose partnership in the ministry of Wholehearted Men is helping to facilitate the breath of God breathing on the dry bones of men's lives across Canada.

Thank you to my precious wife Anne, whose love and prayers support and empower me far more than I have the capacity to comprehend.

Thank you to all the courageous men who have attended our Band of Brothers Boot Camps and Wholehearted Men's Conferences searching for more of the God-Breathed wholeheartedness that Jesus promised us. It has been a great privilege and pleasure to see you come to life and stand up on your feet together, a vast army.

INTRODUCTION

Have you ever wondered why life is so difficult? Is this as good as it gets? Do you think we can expect more, or is this all we can hope for?

Do you believe God really is good, or deep down do you question that? How do you feel about yourself? Are you just a big mess case?

Are you still looking for the abundant life and freedom Jesus promised us? Are there issues in your life you just can't seem to get on top of? Do you feel oppressed and don't understand why?

If any of this resonates with you, you are not alone. Many Christians feel this way. The reality is, there is a very real yet unseen spiritual battle raging all around you. In fact, the story of your life involves a violent and sustained strategy of an unseen enemy who since your conception is actively working to steal, kill and destroy all the life God has for you.

However, most people are completely unaware of this strategy, or even of the reality of this spiritual opposition.

This book is written to help you understand the nature of the spiritual opposition set against you, the simple yet diabolically effective strategy implemented by the enemy of your soul, and the profoundly powerful Tools of Truth Jesus has equipped you with to overcome the spiritual oppression set against you.

Don't simply read this book. Live this book. Practice the Truth contained in this book and your life will be transformed. You can begin to experience freedom from the oppression of the enemy and experience the life Jesus has for you.

Yes, there is more for you. What you have been experiencing is not as good as it gets. You can expect more. God is good and you are not just a big mess case.

There is far more life for you in Jesus, but you have to fight for it. You have to 'appropriate' what He has purchased for you. You can overcome the spiritual oppression set against you and live the life Jesus promised us.

I am pleased to take this journey with you. So let the journey begin...

Strength and courage,

Dave

More information on Dave's work can be found at the following websites:

www.Wholeheartedmen.com

www.Wholeheartedleaders.com

THE STRANGLER FIG

We stood there amidst the glory and splendor of the Costa Rican rainforest gazing up at this diabolical epiphyte. It was so...sinister. Yes, that was it – sinister. Our biologist guide had led us to this particular tree and explained the strategy for its existence.

At the conclusion of his presentation I felt like I had just captured a glimpse into the mindset of a mass murderer, a despotic dictator or a sinister sadist whose sole aim was to inflict a slow, painful, merciless death upon its prey. I was overcome by what appeared as a brutal, unemotional intention to kill.

This was not a side effect, an afterthought, or an infrequent accidental occurrence. No, this was its sole intention: to kill.

I stood there aghast in a holy moment knowing there was more to this lesson than our guide had intended. My eyes had seen this incredible example of creation, but now the Creator was about to teach me a deeper life lesson of an even more diabolical nature...

Our family, my wife Anne and our sons David and Benjamin, had travelled to the wondrous mountain rain forests of Costa Rica to study the glory of God's creation. We wanted to somehow learn more about our Lord by studying the nature of what He had spoken into being. We hired a biologist who had been leading us through the rainforest explaining the incredible complexities found in its various life forms, both flora and fauna.

At this point in our tour he indicated that he wanted to show us one of the most extraordinary trees found in the rainforest. We followed him along a winding path surrounded by trees towering above our heads in an overwhelming canopy of color and life. We stopped at a bizarre looking tree he identified as a Strangler Fig.

The trunk of the Strangler Fig was actually comprised of what appeared to be a hollow lattice-work of thick branches. The tree's scope and size was equal to that of the magnificent trees surrounding us. In fact, it looked much the same as the other trees in the rainforest, except for its unusual trunk. My sons were actually able to squeeze through a larger opening in the lattice-work trunk and stand inside the tree like they were trapped inside an organic prison cell of some kind. They even began to climb up the tree on the inside as the lattice-work of thick branches making up the trunk made for a natural ladder of sorts.

Our guide then began to explain to us the nature of this tree and how it operates. The seed of the Strangler Fig is deposited in the canopy of a healthy rainforest tree, typically by a bird. That tiny seed settles into a crook in the top of the tree and begins to root itself in. As it grows it sends shoots down the length of the trunk of its host tree until they eventually reach the ground.

Once the shoots reach the ground they root into the rich soil and begin providing the nutrients needed by the Strangler Fig to grow at an extraordinary rate. And grow at an extraordinary rate it does. The shoots grow and begin to wrap themselves around the trunk of the healthy host rainforest tree.

The foliage of the Strangler Fig in the canopy of its host tree also begins to grow significantly. The foliage grows to such an extent it cuts off the sunlight feeding the host tree. The shoots grow ever-more large as they entangle the trunk of the host tree in an anaconda-like embrace of death. This deadly embrace continues until the host tree is literally choked and starved to death.

The giant Strangler Fig has now killed its host to stand immense and powerful in the rainforest as a hollow representation of the healthy rainforest tree's former glory. The original tree is dead and gone. In its place is the 'empty' Strangler Fig, an unreasonable facsimile of the now deceased grand and glorious tree.

Diabolical. Deadly. Demonic.

Demonic – really?

Yes, this was the lesson I was about to learn from the Creator about the spiritual opposition set against us...

WARFARE IS UPON US

As we stood there awed, amazed, astounded and aghast at this incredible wonder of creation, the Creator began to whisper to my heart,

"This is a picture of the strategy of the enemy set against my people", I sensed the Lord say.

What? What does that mean?

That was all He said. At least, that's all I heard.

I needed to spend more time drilling into what this meant; what the Lord wanted to say to me. The Strangler Fig is somehow a picture of the spiritual opposition set against us...Lord, help me to understand what this means.

So, let's back this bus up a bit to ensure we have a shared understanding of what I mean by spiritual opposition. In order to do that, I want to look at a few scriptures. Scripture clearly tells us we have a spiritual enemy:

Jesus said in John 10:10

> "The thief comes only to steal, kill, and destroy; I have come that they may have life, and have it to the full."

He was indicating that we have a spiritual enemy whose intention is to harm us. Not simply harm us though - steal, kill and destroy us. Jesus came to offer us life, but our enemy is utterly opposed to that happening.

So, who is our enemy?

1 Peter 5:8 tells us,

> "Be self-controlled and alert. Your enemy the devil prowls around like a roaring lion looking for someone to devour."

The Bible is very clear there is a spiritual realm populated with angels, and fallen angels called demons. All angels were created as glorious spirit beings in fellowship with God. They were given free will, and Satan/Lucifer in his free will became proud, wanting to be worshipped instead of God. So, he instigated a rebellion against God and led one third of the angels in a war against God and the angels,

Ezekiel 28:12b-14, 17

"You were the model of perfection, full of wisdom and perfect in beauty... every precious stone adorned you: ruby, topaz and emerald, chrysolite, onyx, and jasper, sapphire, turquoise and beryl... You were anointed as guardian of the cherub, for so I ordained you. You were on the holy mount of God;... Your heart became proud on account of your beauty, and you corrupted your wisdom because of your splendor. So I threw you to the earth;"

Isaiah 14:12-15

"How you have fallen from heaven, O morning star, son of the dawn! You have been cast down to the earth, you who once laid low the nations! You said in your heart, 'I will ascend to heaven; I will raise my throne above the stars of God; I will sit enthroned on the mount of assembly, on the utmost heights of the sacred mountain... I will make myself like the Most High.' But you are brought down to the grave, to the depths of the pit."

Revelation 12:3-9

"Then another sign appeared in heaven: an enormous red dragon with seven heads and ten horns and seven crowns on its heads. Its tail swept a third of the stars out of the sky and flung them to the earth. The dragon stood in front of the woman who was about to give birth, so that it might devour her child the moment he was born. She gave birth to a son, a male child, who "will rule all the nations with an iron scepter." And her child was snatched up to God and to his throne. The woman fled into the wilderness to a place prepared for her by God, where she might be taken care of for 1,260 days.

Then war broke out in heaven. Michael and his angels fought against the dragon, and the dragon and his angels fought back. But he was not strong enough, and they lost their place in heaven. The great dragon was hurled down—that ancient serpent called the devil, or Satan, who leads the whole world astray. He was hurled to the earth, and his angels with him."

So what does this mean for you?

Well, it is critically important you understand you have been born into battle. There is a war going on in the spirit realm that impacts you on a daily basis. As Jesus says in John 10, we have an enemy who is out to steal, kill and destroy all the abundant life Jesus has for us. If we do not understand the nature of the spiritual battle going on all around us we end up believing two things:

1. God is a bad God

2. I am a bad person

However, there is a third position we must understand: we have an enemy who has declared war against us and wants to ruin our lives and all the life God has for us.

Revelation 12:17

> "Then the dragon was enraged at the woman and went off to make war against the rest of her offspring – those who obey God's commandment and hold to the testimony of Jesus."

Have you ever found yourself asking, "Why is life so hard? Why are things so difficult? Is this as good as it gets? I thought Jesus came that we might have abundant life – if this is abundant life I must be missing something…"

Life can be difficult sometimes can't it? Well, it's even more difficult if we don't understand we have an enemy in the spirit realm that is dead set against us. Just like Aragorn said to King Théoden in The Two Towers, "Open war is upon you whether you would risk it or not."

Scripture is very clear about this spiritual battle:

Ephesians 6:12

> "For our struggle is not against flesh and blood, but against the rulers, against the authorities, against the powers of this dark world and against the spiritual forces of evil in the heavenly realms."

What makes this battle so difficult is that our enemy is unseen. Our enemy is in the spirit realm, so we must see with different eyes. However, the first step in winning this fight is actually to understand there is a fight going on and you are in it whether you want to be or not.

Sun Tsu in the Art of War said that the highest form of warfare is to defeat your enemy in his mind before he ever takes the battle field. However, I believe he is wrong. The highest form of warfare is to convince your enemy that he does not have an enemy.

That is what our enemy has done.

"The finest trick of the devil is to persuade you that he does not exist." Charles Baudelaire

That jig is now up though: we see we have a spiritual enemy and it's time to step into the reality of that understanding.

APPROPRIATE LIFE

Have you ever been in a physical fight in total darkness? I have and it's no fun I can tell you that.

When I was about 11 years old we went to my cousins' house for Christmas. I asked my uncle where Calvin and Roy were. He said they were downstairs waiting to show me what they got for Christmas. So, innocently I raced downstairs into the family room announcing my arrival.

When I got into the room I couldn't see my older cousins, but suddenly the door closed behind me and the lights turned off.

"Hey guys, what's going on?", I hesitantly inquired.

"We want to show you what we got for Christmas – boxing gloves!", came the reply.

And with that I began to receive blow after blow from my unseen assailants, feeling quite powerless to fight back because I was outnumbered, outgunned and I couldn't see where the punches were coming from.

Life can feel like that sometimes can't it? We keep taking hits with no idea where they are coming from, how to protect ourselves and how to stop it. It's no fun is it?

Like I indicated earlier, we end up believing God is really not good, and we are totally messed up. We can lose heart and end up living a substandard life instead of the abundant life Jesus offers us.

Now that we understand there is a spiritual battle raging all around us to prevent us from apprehending, from 'appropriating', all the life that Jesus promised us, what do we do?

We must understand that the life Jesus promised us and purchased for us through His death on the cross and resurrection from the dead doesn't just land in our lap. It doesn't simply miraculously appear. We are miraculously born again by the redemptive work of the Holy Spirit, but we must then begin to work out our salvation. Not trying to earn our salvation, but to get hold of what Jesus purchased for us and what he is inviting us into:

Philippians 2:12

> "Therefore, my dear friends, as you have always obeyed—not only in my presence, but now much more in my absence—continue to work out your salvation with fear and trembling,"

We have to 'appropriate' the freedom, life, healing, and wholeness Jesus bought for us. To "appropriate" means to "take hold of", "to own". God is not a divine vending machine here to serve us as customers - to simply drop what we want into our laps. We must choose to live differently. We must choose to think differently. We must choose to believe differently. What we believe determines how we think and how we live.

And here is the wonder of God's work in us: as we work to appropriate all that our salvation has purchased us, God works in us and through us to live differently. God empowers us to live according to His will and His way…

Philippians 2:13

> "For it is God who works in you to will and to act according to his good purpose."

So what stops us from walking in our glory and calling - in all that Jesus has for us? What stops us from walking with Jesus into the freedom, life, healing, wholeness, restoration, etc. that He has for us?

We have to fight for it. We have to appropriate it. We have to press on to take hold of it. Salvation is free, but the Kingdom of God (the Rule of God, the Government of God – the way God meant us to live) costs us our life.

Philippians 3:12

> "Not that I have already obtained all this, or have already been made perfect, but I press on to take hold of that for which Christ Jesus took hold of me."

We must make two critical commitments and take two critical actions:

1. Surrender and fight
2. Believe the Truth, not the lies

Your victory begins with surrender. Jesus invites you to surrender your life to Him,

Matthew 10:39

> "Whoever finds their life will lose it, and whoever loses their life for my sake will find it."

As Deitrich Bonhoeffer said, "Jesus beckons us to come and die."

Not my will Lord, but yours be done. Jesus isn't here to serve you, you are here to serve Him.

So what does that look like?

SURRENDER AND FIGHT

Did you ever see the movie the Karate Kid – the original version? Daniel is a teenager who is getting beaten up at school by a group of guys who use their karate skills to bully others. Daniel is sick and tired of getting whipped so he looks into taking karate, and discovers the caretaker of the apartment he and his mom live in is a Japanese expert in karate – Mr. Miyagi.

Mr. Miyagi agrees to teach him karate and invites Daniel to come by his home every Saturday morning to learn karate. What Daniel ends up learning is how to "wax on, wax off" the cars, "sand the floor" of his decks, "paint the fence" and "paint the house" according to the technique outlined by the Japanese master.

After working another exhausting day doing what appears to be chores around Mr. Miyagi's house while Mr. Miyagi was out fishing, Daniel, at his breaking point, lets loose on his so-called sensei. Daniel vehemently complains about the fact that he wanted to learn karate and all he has been doing for weeks is working around the house. He's fed up and announces he is quitting what he deems to be useless activity and nothing to do with his goal of learning karate.

Mr. Miyagi then commands Daniel to stay and demonstrate "wax on, wax off", "paint the house", "sand the floor", and "paint the fence". Unbeknownst to Daniel, all the techniques he learned in the midst of the drudgery of work were actually karate moves effectively teaching him the lessons he had eagerly desired. He did not recognize what was going on until he submitted to the master.

We are no different. Often what we may deem to be life's difficulties, from which we want to be rescued, are actually situations the Lord is using to train us, to discover if we are willing to surrender to Him and trust Him in the midst of the difficulties. Our victory begins with surrender to the Master, and our surrender begins with our humility:

James 4:6b, 7

> "'God opposes the proud but gives grace to the humble.' Submit yourselves then to God, resist the devil and he will flee from you."

Our life in Jesus and our victory over the strategy of the enemy begins with surrender. Authority *in* Jesus begins with surrender *to* Jesus. True authority ultimately begins with humility.

Jesus told us that He has all authority in Heaven and on earth, as we do in His name. Our authority over the enemy, our victory, rests in the authority of Christ and our surrender to His Lordship.

Years ago during a prayer meeting I saw a picture in my mind as I prayed. I was hiking up a mountain trail wearing a large expeditionary back pack. The pack was full with everything I believed I needed for the journey ahead of me. I came to a fork in the path with one path going up the mountain and another heading down to the valley.

At the fork stood Jesus. He was holding a climbing rope and a climbing axe. He asked me to give Him my back pack in exchange for the rope and axe. He indicated that was really what I needed. My first thought was that I couldn't give Him my pack because it contained everything I needed for my trip.

The picture ended.

Over the course of a number of months the Lord helped me understand what this meant. The rope represented the Word of God – Truth. The climbing axe represented the Holy Spirit – the Spirit of Truth. My back pack represented all the things I wanted to accomplish in this life in order for me to feel like I had lived a successful life:

- A great house in a great neighbourhood
- Good vehicles
- A boat
- Great work that contributed to the betterment of our community
- A good reputation in the community
- International mission travel
- Good family holidays

- A great marriage with great kids
- A good level of income to obtain all this and contribute to the work of the Kingdom
- Etc., etc.

Jesus was calling me to surrender all of this, all my hopes and dreams, to follow Him depending on His Word and the Holy Spirit. He had to be enough for me – period.

This was the beginning of what I called the School of Brokenness and Surrender for me. Jesus was beckoning me to come and die so that I might truly live in Him. He was calling me to surrender to Him - to submit to His authority so that I could live in His authority.

This is what He calls all of us to - surrender to God so that we might appropriate the life He has for us and overcome the spiritual opposition set against us.

Your victory begins with your surrender. Your life begins with your death. We must submit to the Master's will and His training in order to fight effectively and overcome the spiritual opposition set against us. Perhaps this means you need to change the way you are praying in the midst of life's difficulties.

Instead of asking Jesus to rescue you *out of* your trials, you need to invite Him *into* your trials. What you want to flee from may very well be the process through which He wants to refine you - to learn to submit and surrender *to* His Authority so you can begin to truly live *in* His authority.

Living in His authority enables you to overcome the spiritual opposition set against you.

So what does the spiritual opposition set against you actually look like?

THE WHISPER CAMPAIGN

As the group of marine recruits jogs past the Gunny Sargent hidden in the bush, they are totally oblivious to what is about to happen. This lesson will be violent, dangerous and one they will never forget. However, it is a lesson they must learn in order to survive.

Their commanding officer steps out of the bush after his unsuspecting victims run past him on the trail. He raises the AK 47 and begins to fire. The bullets zip past them and amongst them causing complete pandemonium, but no physical damage, as they dive for cover.

After the shooting stops and they come out from hiding, the lesson is delivered with crystal clarity,

"This is the AK 47 assault rifle – the preferred weapon of your enemy. It makes a distinct sound when fired upon you, so learn to recognize it!"

Wow.

When I saw that scene from the movie Heartbreak Ridge with Clint Eastwood, the Lord tapped me on the shoulder and let me know this is a profound truth I need to understand. Do I recognize the sound of enemy fire in my life? Am I able to recognize when I am being shot at in the spirit? Oftentimes what I think is just a bad day, a bad mood, or the remnants of a bad sleep, is actually enemy fire.

So what does that look like? If we are going to effectively fight the spiritual enemy who is out to steal, kill and destroy us then we need to know how he attacks us. We need to discern the sound of enemy fire.

How does our spiritual enemy attack us? What is his strategy set against you to stop you from appropriating all the life that God has for you and through you to others in your life?

I call it the Whisper Campaign.

What did Jesus tell us about our enemy? We have already seen what He said about the nature of our enemy and his objective, but now we need to understand his strategy.

When speaking to those who opposed His message, Jesus gives us a profound glimpse into the nature and strategy of our enemy:

John 8:44

> "You belong to your father, the devil, and you want to carry out your father's desire. He was a murderer from the beginning, not holding to the truth, for there is no truth in him. When he lies, he speaks his native language, for he is a liar and the father of lies."

Revelation 12:10

> "Then I heard a loud voice in heaven say: 'Now have come the salvation and the power and the kingdom of our God, and the authority of his Christ. For the accuser of our brothers, who accuses them before our God day and night, has been hurled down.'"

Quite simply, our spiritual enemy - the demonic host - lies to us constantly and consistently. That's the Whisper Campaign. Whispering lies into our hearts and minds to keep us from believing what God says.

The demonic realm under the command and direction of Satan implements a very effective spiritual Whisper Campaign of lies and deceit intended to keep God's people from believing the Truth. It is the same strategy implemented in the Garden of Eden. The strategy of the spiritual opposition set against us is to get us to believe lies, not the Truth.

Living the abundant life Jesus has for us is utterly and completely dependent on us believing the Truth and living the Truth:

John 8:31, 32

> "To the Jews who had believed him, Jesus said, 'If you hold to my teaching, you are really my disciples. Then you will know the truth, and the truth will set you free.'"

John 14:6

> "Jesus answered, 'I am the way and the truth and the life. No one comes to the Father except through me.'"

John 16:13

> "But when he, the Spirit of truth, comes, he will guide you into all the truth. He will not speak on his own; he will speak only what he hears, and he will tell you what is yet to come."

3 John 4

> "I have no greater joy than to hear that my children are walking in the Truth."

Jesus is the Truth. Jesus promised to send and baptize us in the Spirit of Truth to guide us in all Truth. Why? Because the Truth will set us free. Knowing the Truth – appropriating the Truth – will set you free. Why will Truth set us free? Because we have been held captive to the lies of the enemy.

The Whisper Campaign of the enemy are those "thoughts" that keep rolling around your mind and heart 24/7 belittling, berating, badgering and bullying:

"Who do you think you are? You have nothing to offer. Nobody really wants you around. God doesn't care about you. You can't trust anyone. No one cares about you. You don't have what it takes. Prayer doesn't work...", etc., etc., etc.

It's demonic Trash Talk.

Your life is the story of an ongoing assault by a spiritual enemy who is utterly opposed to you experiencing all the life Jesus has for you. So, starting at conception you have been the target of a Whisper Campaign of lies sent from the pit of hell.

Our enemy is very clever indeed. He lies and accuses. He lies to us about who God is, who he is, who we are, and who other people in our lives are. He has convinced most of the world that he doesn't even exist, that God is a bad God and that we are bad people.

It is easy to lead someone into sin if they don't know who they are and don't know who God is. Who do you believe you are? Who do you believe God is?

This is the same strategy he used when he tempted Jesus:

Luke 4:3-9

> "...If you are the son of God...turn these stones to bread...if you are the son of God...throw yourself down..."

This came right after God had spoken to Jesus at his baptism,

Mark 1:11 (The Message)

"You are my Son, chosen and marked by my love, pride of my life."

Our enemy is a very shrewd, cunning and diabolical liar and his objective is to get us to believe something about ourselves that is not the truth and to believe something about God that is not the truth.

We must choose to believe the Truth and not the lies. We must learn to recognize enemy fire in our lives. We must understand how the "Spiritual Strangler Fig" works...

THE SPIRITUAL STRANGLER FIG

Do you remember the story of the Strangler Fig and that the Lord said to me this was a picture of how our enemy works in our lives? Well, here is the strategy of our enemy, how the Whisper Campaign works and how the Spiritual Strangler Fig keeps you from the abundant life Jesus has for you.

The enemy, through the Whisper Campaign, drops a lie into your heart. If we do not identify that thought as a lie and throw it out, it begins to grow in our hearts just like the seed of the Strangler Fig.

Scripture exhorts us to guard our hearts,

Proverbs 4:23

> "Above all else guard your heart for from it flows the wellspring of life."

A primary way we guard our hearts is to take captive the thoughts that enter our minds and hearts:

2 Corinthians 10:3-5

> "For though we live in the world, we do not wage war as the world does. The weapons we fight with are not the weapons of the world. On the contrary, they have divine power to demolish strongholds. We demolish arguments and every pretension that sets itself up against the knowledge of God, and we take captive every thought to make it obedient to Christ."

We must ensure we are thinking about and dwelling on the Truth, not the lies of the enemy.

If we do not identify the lies of the enemy being whispered into our hearts we let them take root and they grow. Like the Strangler Fig they effectively grow and begin to choke out the life God has for us. We slowly die at a deep heart level and end up becoming hollow representations of the people God created us to be. We have been robbed of the Truth that sets us free and are captive to the lies of the enemy sent to steal, kill and destroy.

As followers of Jesus we find ourselves wondering why we are not experiencing the abundant life Jesus promised us. Why is life so hard? Why do I feel so empty? Is this as good as it gets? Is this all I can hope for? This isn't how it was supposed to be – where is all the abundant life Jesus promised me?

Well, if that is how you are feeling and thinking there is a spiritual strangler fig squeezing the life out of you. The lies of the enemy are robbing you of the life Jesus has for you.

Here is the process of how the enemy works in our hearts – understanding this and working through the Tools of Truth I will show you in the following chapters will completely change your life.

Wound – Lie – Agreement – Vow – False Self

Starting back to when you were conceived, the enemy implemented this strategy. You have experienced wounding at a heart level throughout your life: hurtful words that were said, or affirming and loving words that were left unsaid; painful things that were done to you or joys taken from you; and all manner of painful circumstances.

In the midst of those times of wounding, when you were vulnerable, the enemy dropped a lie into your heart. You made an agreement with that lie. You then made a vow to be a certain way. That vow shifted you from being who you truly are to being a "false self" – someone you weren't created to be.

Let me illustrate with something I have had to work through in my life:

When I was 9 years old my mother died. It was a tragedy that significantly impacted my entire family. I remember the day we were waiting at the hospital when the doctor informed us mom had passed away – "I am sorry Mr. MacLean, there was nothing we could do.", announced the doctor.

My brother, sister, father and I returned from the hospital mourning deeply - we were all broken. My brother and sister who were 19 and 20 at the time raced up to their bedrooms to weep in private. I sat on the living room sofa crying while dad phoned relatives in the kitchen to let them know mom had died.

I was all alone desperately hoping someone would comfort me and let me know things were going to be alright. I was crying so loudly that dad called up to my sister to come down and comfort me so he could continue doing what he thought was the right thing to do. She was caught up in her own grief and did not come. Dad was caught up in his own grief doing what he thought was best.

So, I sat there alone, broken-hearted weeping uncontrollably in my brokenness. In the midst of my woundedness, completely unbeknownst to me – my family did not know Jesus or have any element of spiritual awareness - the enemy engaged in a very effective whisper campaign:

"Nobody notices you. Nobody cares. You are all alone. You can't count on anyone."

These were the lies that were deposited in my heart. This was the Spiritual Strangler Fig taking root. This was the demonic Whisper Campaign.

Those lies (thoughts) made total sense to me, so I agreed with them. I made an agreement with the enemy to believe those lies – again, completely subconsciously.

I then made some very significant vows:

"If I can't count on anyone then I don't need anyone! And, if nobody notices me, then from now on I will make sure that everyone notices me!"

How did that change me? What was my false self that was formed? Well, I became an independent, isolated and emotionally insulated person who would not let anyone get too close. And, I became a shameless self-promoter who needed to be noticed and needed to be very popular.

The Spiritual Strangler Fig took root and began to squeeze the life out of me. I was believing lies, not the Truth.

I met Jesus years later in a profound and powerful way, but it was not until years after that when I began to understand how the enemy had planted lies in my heart during times of woundedness all throughout my life – particularly in my childhood. Once I understood the strategy of the enemy I began to unpack these experiences to invite the Lord to bring healing and freedom.

When the Lord spoke to me in Costa Rica through the Strangler Fig I realized I needed to identify the lies of the enemy, the Spiritual Strangler Fig, which had encompassed my heart and had been squeezing the life out of me.

That leads us to the next step in our journey to freedom…

Your Book of Lies

Walking along a long black sand beach on the Pacific Coast of Costa Rica I began to ask the Lord to help me see how invasive the lies of the enemy were in my heart. Through this revelation of the Spiritual Strangler Fig He had invited me on a journey of discovery and freedom. I knew there was more He wanted to show me, but I also knew I needed to wrestle with this in order to get hold of the Truth – to appropriate what Jesus had for me.

I thought it would be good to begin to make note of the lies I had believed over the years. So, I took my journal, flipped it open to a fresh page and wrote at the top, "My Book of Lies". I then asked the Lord to help me see the lies I have believed...

When I speak on this topic at Wholehearted Men's conferences I read my book of lies to the men in attendance. I ask them to raise their hand if they have believed at least one of the lies that I had believed. Every hand in the room goes up. I then ask the men to look around and see that they are not the only one dealing with this. The penny drops: "Hey, I am not the only one dealing with this." In fact, this is a strategy used by our enemy on everyone – no one is exempt.

You are not alone. You are not the only one dealing with whatever you are dealing with. Your enemy simply wants you to believe that, but it's a lie.

The Whisper Campaign is incessant, insipid, diabolical and deadly.

It is also very simple. The strategy of the enemy – his Whisper Campaign, his Spiritual Strangler Fig – has 2 primary objectives:

1. Divide and, 2. Conquer.

The enemy's lies are sent to Divide us and Conquer us.

The Dividing objective in the whisper campaign is comprised of lies sent to alienate and isolate you:

"You don't belong. No one cares. No one wants you around. You are all alone. You don't need anyone. You can't trust anyone. You can't trust God.", etc. These lies are meant to alienate and isolate you from Christian community – from your allies in this battle. They are designed to get you living life alone – away from the input of others; away from the input of people who can help bring Truth into your situation.

Dividing lies separate you from Christian community which makes you even more vulnerable to Conquering lies. Like Clint Eastwood said, "A man alone is easy prey."

The first tactic in destroying you and your faith is to get you alienated and isolated.

The Conquering objective in the whisper campaign is comprised of lies sent to demean and diminish you:

"You are not good enough. You are not smart enough. You are not talented enough. You don't have what it takes. You will ultimately fail. You have nothing to offer. You are a loser. You are a failure. You are trapped. You are a bad leader. You are weak and small. You are insignificant.", etc.

These lies destroy your faith, hope, courage, strength, and freedom – your very life. Your spiritual enemy's ultimate objective is to destroy you. That is very tough to do if you are walking in community with other people – allies - who believe the Truth and are walking with Jesus filled with the Spirit of Truth. The input of your allies counteracts the lies of the enemy.

However, when you start walking alone feeling alienated and isolated, you will begin to swallow hook, line and sinker the lies sent to demean and diminish you. Soon you have no faith, hope or strength left, and you will have been conquered.

So, knowing you are probably struggling with many of the same lies that I have struggled with, I share my Book of Lies with you to help you see the extent of the Spiritual Strangler Fig in your heart:

Dividing Lies:

- No one notices me
- No one cares
- I am all alone
- I can't count on anyone
- I don't belong
- It's up to me to make it happen
- God doesn't care
- I don't need anyone
- No one really wants or needs me

Conquering Lies:

- I have to win to be acceptable, loved or significant
- I am not good enough
- "This" is not good enough
- My wife isn't good enough
- My kids aren't good enough
- My work isn't good enough
- Nothing I have ever done is good enough
- I have to be perfect or everything gets taken away
- I have to be a hero
- I will never be a hero
- I have to make a big difference
- I can't really make a difference
- Prayer doesn't work
- Things will never change or get better
- I am trapped
- I have nothing of value to offer others
- I don't have what it takes to follow Jesus
- I am a bad leader and when I lead I just hurt people
- I have to be great
- I will never be great
- I am small and always will be
- I will ultimately fail and lose everything
- I have no greater glory
- I am an under achiever and always will be

- I am disqualified from God's "A" Team
- God isn't really engaged in my life
- God won't be good unless I am good
- I can't trust God to be good
- This is as good as it gets

OK, raise your hand if you have believed at least one of these lies. Of course you have. The enemy who has declared war on you has been working since you have been born to steal, kill and destroy – to keep you from all the life and freedom Jesus has for you. He uses imperfect people in our lives who cause wounding, but the real enemy is in the spirit realm. It's not the imperfect people in our lives who unfortunately hurt us that are the enemy, it's the demonic realm who take advantage of those circumstances to enslave us with lies.

Every one of the lies in my book of lies is tied to some sort of wounding that involved another person in my life. A parent, a sibling, a relative, a friend, a teacher, a stranger, the enemy uses a vast array of imperfect broken people in our lives to ensnare us in his Spiritual Strangler Fig and squeeze the life out of us.

It's time for you to write your own book of lies. Don't feel shame. Don't feel condemnation. You were taken advantage of by a cowardly, uncreative enemy in the midst of your vulnerability and ignorance. When you write out your book of lies see if you can put the lies you have believed into 2 categories: 1. Dividing lies sent to alienate and isolate you; 2. Conquering lies sent to demean and diminish you.

Before I let you go to write your book of lies I want to address one lie in particular that can hamstring many believers,

"Your sin disqualifies you from walking with Jesus. You are a disappointment so don't think you can do anything particularly worthwhile. Just sit down and shut up and try not to screw up too badly."

Lies!

Do you know it's not your sin that disqualifies you? That's right. The only thing that disqualifies you is pride. Why? Because pride will prevent you from repenting and receiving the grace, mercy and forgiveness of God. So, in an attempt to help you understand the Truth in regard to that particular lie I want to outline for you the qualifications for partnering with Jesus in this epic adventure called the Kingdom of God – the 5 qualifications for life in Christ:

1. You must be Weak and Foolish – I Corinthians 1:27, "But God chose the foolish things of the world to shame the wise; God chose the weak things of the world to shame the strong."
2. You must be a Sinner – Matthew 9:13, "…for I have not come to call the righteous, but sinners."
3. You must be willing to Humble yourself – I Peter 5:5,6, "God opposes the proud but shows favor to the humble. Humble yourselves, therefore, under God's mighty hand, that he may lift you up in due time."
4. You must be willing to Repent – Acts 3:19, "Repent, then, and turn to God, so that your sins may be wiped out, that times of refreshing may come from the Lord."
5. You must Believe the Truth – Mark 1:15, "The time has come," he said. "The kingdom of God has come near. Repent and believe the good news!"

Is that great news or what?! You bet that's great news!!!!

We are now going to shift gears and discover how we can pull out the Spiritual Strangler Figs in our heart – how we can get free from the lies of the enemy and break the power of the Whisper Campaign.

But we can't do that until you identify the lies of the enemy that have taken root in your heart, so start writing your book of lies. Take a break right now. Ask the Lord to help you see what you have believed that is not the Truth…

The Tools of Truth

Have you ever seen the movie The Truman Show? It is an amazing depiction of the Whisper Campaign of the enemy.

It's the story of Truman, played by Jim Carey, who as a baby was adopted by a movie production company and raised on television 24/7 in the world's largest studio. The studio is an actual seaside town – all fabricated of course. Everyone in Truman's life is an actor. Truman is lied to his entire life, but he thinks everything is very real.

He does at least until, as a man, something begins to stir in his heart. He begins to think there must be something more to life than the small existence he is living. At this time he is married and at the beginning of his career as an insurance salesman.

Truman's inner stirring is unsettling to the creator and producer of the show who wants to ensure Truman keeps living his controlled, contrived and contained life. The producer wants him to keep living a small existence within the elaborate seaside village set they have created, which is in fact, Truman's prison. He wants to ensure Truman remains completely oblivious to the reality of life and the 'great cloud of witnesses' watching the show on TV 24/7.

What a profound picture of the strategy of the enemy in our life. Our enemy wants to keep us living a very small story, trapped in a world of lies not knowing there is freedom beyond our wildest imagination outside the walls of our cage. At one point in the show when Truman is beginning to awaken to the Truth that there is life outside of his small story the producer comments,

"He (Truman) could leave at any time if his was more than a vague ambition. If he was absolutely determined to discover the truth there is no way we could prevent him…Truman prefers his 'cell'."

This is our reality as well. If we are committed to getting free there is no way the enemy can stop us. Jesus purchased our freedom through His death and resurrection.

Galatians 5:1

> "It is for freedom that Christ has set us free. Stand firm then and do not let yourselves be burdened again by a yoke of slavery to sin."

We too have a great cloud of witnesses cheering us to freedom, to fight the good fight,

Hebrews 12:1-2

> "Therefore, since we are surrounded by such a great cloud of witnesses, let us throw off everything that hinders and the sin that so easily entangles, and let us run with perseverance the race marked out for us. Let us fix our eyes on Jesus, the author and perfecter of our faith, who for the joy set before him endured the cross, scorned its shame, and sat down at the right hand of the throne of God."

By the way, do you know what the 'joy set before Jesus' is? You. And me. Us. It's God's people being set free from the chains of the enemy to live in all the fullness of the life of God, the Kingdom of God, in us and through us. Yes, we are the joy of the Lord, and it's for freedom that He set us free, so let's stop believing the lies of the enemy and believe the Truth.

How do we pull up the Spiritual Strangler Fig in our hearts? How do we break free from the lies of the enemy? There are 5 Tools of Truth we must implement. In fact, we must choose to walk in these Tools of Truth every day if we want to appropriate all Jesus has purchased for us.

If we truly want to see God's Kingdom come and His will be done in us and through us, then we must choose to live this way. These tools of truth will enable you to break free from the lies of the enemy and deal with the lies of the enemy on an ongoing basis.

The 5 Tools of Truth:
1. Repent
2. Renounce
3. Rebuke
4. Receive
5. Rejoice

I want to ensure you understand that what you are about to read is not a panacea. It is not a cure all. It is not the recipe to total freedom. I believe this is a powerful Truth to empower you to live in increasing freedom. However, this little booklet does not contain all Truth. This is simply what I call a Trickle of Truth God has shared with me that is one Tributary of Truth from the river of God's complete Truth.

John Eldredge in his book Waking the Dead provides us with a profound teaching about what he calls the "4 Streams of Ministry" we need in the church:
1. Counselling
2. Inner Healing
3. Warfare
4. Discipleship

Over the decades I have walked with Jesus I have benefited from all of these streams. I have been significantly impacted from these ministries that wonderful people have provided to me and others. This teaching on the lies of the enemy and the Tools of Truth provides you with some insight into warfare and discipleship, but there is still much, much more God has for you to set you free to live the life Jesus has purchased for you.

You may recall in the movie The Matrix there is a scene where Neo encounters an agent in the subway. Normally when Neo or any other of the crew of the Nebuchadnezzar encounters an agent, they run away. However, this time is different. Neo has been discovering there is far more to him and his power than the agents had led him to believe. When confronted he does not run. He turns and faces the agent. He chooses to stay and fight.

Trinity, one of his shipmates who is looking on at what is happening from the safety of their ship asks this question to Morpheus, their leader:

"What is he doing?"

Morpheus' reply is what I am hoping you have been doing as you are reading this book:

"He is beginning to believe!"

It's time to believe the Truth, not the lies. To fight the enemy and pull out the Spiritual Strangler Fig sent to steal, kill and destroy us. Let us begin working through the 5 Tools of Truth...

Repent

Do you golf? I golf a little. I get bored after 9 holes though so I don't golf 18 holes. However, my claim to fame is that I have golfed Pebble Beach. Not only did I golf it, but I parred it. Yup, that's right. I shot par at Pebble Beach. Pretty impressive for a guy who rarely golfs eh?!

Hold on, I sense that you don't really believe me. It is true that I shot par at Pebble Beach – I promise. However, I actually played Pebble Beach on a golf simulator in a hotel in Seattle. It was an amazing experience: a massive screen displayed in HD quality the exact hole at Pebble Beach I was playing, complete with trees swaying gently in the breeze. I would hit a real golf ball with the club of my choosing at the screen where the trajectory of my shot would be calculated immediately by computer. I would watch as my ball displayed on the screen landing where it would have if I had actually shot a ball on the course.

On the small computer terminal where I controlled a number of variables of the game including club selection, and the hole I was playing, was a button that made my great game at Pebble Beach possible – it was called "Mulligan".

For those of you who don't play golf you need to know that "Mulligan" is a golf term for not counting a shot. If you hit a terrible shot and don't want it to count against you, you call a Mulligan. Now, of course, this cannot be utilized in professional play, but amongst friends you typically come to an agreement about Mulligans. Perhaps you can claim 1 "Mully" on the front nine holes and 1 on the back nine.

On this day though, I granted myself unlimited Mulligans. If I hit a bad shot I would press the Mulligan button and that shot would not count against me. I would then adjust my grip, my stance, my swing angle, and shoot again. Good shots I would keep, errant shots I would claim a Mulligan.

I tell you this story because it is a beautiful depiction of repentance. Repentance is God's gift of forgiveness to us - not counting our sin against us. Repentance is a Miraculous Mulligan, a Divine Do Over, and a Spiritual Start Again.

1 John 1:9

> "If we confess our sins He is faithful and just to forgive our sins and cleanse us from all unrighteousness."

Why does our journey to freedom from the lies of the enemy begin with repentance? Well, because we chose to believe a lie instead of the Truth. We believed what the enemy whispered to us instead of what God told us was true.

God forgives us when we confess our sins, it is His gift of grace through the work of Christ on the cross.

This may be an area where you have believed another lie of the enemy. "God can't really forgive you. You don't deserve it. What you have done is too bad to forgive."

Not believing that Jesus can forgive you is arrogance. Somehow what Jesus accomplished through his death and resurrection was good enough for everyone else, but not for you. Jesus died once for *all* sins – that's the truth. Receive His forgiveness.

I Peter 3:18

> "For Christ died for sins once for all, the righteous for the unrighteous, to bring you to God."

Repenting begins with a prayer of confession like this:

"Lord, please forgive me for believing the lie of the enemy. I know this must grieve you. Please forgive me and cleanse me from all unrighteousness."

When you do this I suggest you name the exact lie you are repenting from. Please keep in mind, confession does not equal repentance, it is merely the first step in repenting. True repentance involves a change in behavior. The following 4 Tools of Truth are the outworking of this initial confession, the outworking of your repentance...

Renounce

I ran my own business for many years. During that time I signed many agreements with our clients. We called the document a "Letter of Agreement". The agreements outlined my firm's obligations and our client's obligations. The gist of the content of the agreement was fairly simple;

 "MacLean Group commits to providing the following services…Client commits to providing the following payment according to the following terms." Agreements contain the terms and conditions agreed upon by the two parties.

Every agreement contained an 'out clause' – how we or the client could get out of the agreement. We could terminate the agreement based on a number of factors. The client could also terminate the agreement based on a number of factors.

To terminate the agreement either party simply needed to present a written declaration they were severing the agreement. Of course, there were then certain obligations that needed to be fulfilled according to the initial agreement, but the out clause provided either party with the authority to renounce the agreement.

To "renounce" simply means, "…to give up or put aside voluntarily; to renounce worldly pleasures; to give up by formal declaration; to renounce a claim…" Synonyms for renounce include, "forsake, forgo, forswear, leave, quit, resign, abdicate, disclaim, reject, disavow, and deny".

The reality is, you made an agreement with the lies of the enemy. He presented you with a lie that you bought into. You agreed with that lie and then made a vow - a commitment to act based on the agreement with the lie.

There are definitely terms and conditions in the agreement you made with the lies of the enemy. And they are very one sided. The payment terms of this agreement are oppressive and crushing. It is a bad agreement and needs to be broken.

The great news is that Jesus purchased your freedom through His death and resurrection. He has broken the power of sin, death and the enemy, so we have an "out clause" in the agreements we made with the enemy.

I Corinthians 15:56-58

> "The sting of death is sin, and the power of sin is the law. But thanks be to God! He gives us the victory through our Lord Jesus Christ. Therefore, my dear brothers, stand firm. Let nothing move you. Always give yourselves fully to the work of the Lord, because you know that your labor in the Lord is not in vain."

Colossians 2:13-15

> "When you were dead in your sins and in the uncircumcision of your sinful nature, God made you alive with Christ. He forgave us all our sins, having canceled the written code, with its regulations, that was against us and that stood opposed to us; he took it away, nailing it to the cross. And having disarmed the powers and authorities, he made a public spectacle of them, triumphing over them by the cross."

Through Jesus you have the authority to renounce the agreement you made with the lies of the enemy and break the power of the vows you made. That is great news! You don't need to stay trapped in a one-sided oppressive agreement anymore. It's as simple as verbally declaring that you renounce the agreement and the vow you made. Tear up the agreement and renounce the vows you made. Say "No!!!! I will not believe this anymore!"

Here is a sample of the kind of prayer you can pray to do this:

"I tear up the agreement I made with the lies of the enemy. I break the power of the agreement in the name and authority of Jesus Christ. I choose to call it a lie, it is not the truth, and I declare that I want nothing to do with this. I also renounce the vow I made in regard to this agreement. I break the agreement and renounce it and the vow I made with this lie and with the enemy in the name and authority of Jesus Christ."

Again, name the specific lie you agreed with and the subsequent vow you made. Now, let's shift gears a little and learn what the next step is in your journey into freedom...

Rebuke

Have you ever been rebuked by someone? It's not a very pleasant experience is it? I remember years ago as a teenager I was riding a crowded gondola up to the top of the mountain to ski. I was a bit of an outspoken, opinionated, cocky and arrogant young man. Some would call it bombastic, some mouthy, but regardless of the term that might be applied to me I was definitely in need of some character refining.

On this occasion, I forget all the exact details of what went on, I said something out loud on the gondola that was a foolish thing for a young man to say. It was just plain stupid. Typically in those types of situations people are too nice to say anything, they just ignore what is said and write it off to the stupidity of youth. However, there was one woman on that gondola who did not adhere to that type of "niceness".

To my surprise, shock and humiliation this woman unloaded on me. She loudly rebuked me in front of everyone. She put me in my place. She was fierce. She was forceful. She was highly effective in her remarks. She was not nice. She gave me what I needed. I stood down and regretted what I had said. She was right and I knew it. She rebuked me good and I have never forgotten that experience.

To rebuke means, "...to express sharp, stern disapproval of; reprove; reprimand..." You cannot rebuke and be timid or nice. To rebuke is to be fierce. It is standing up in strength. To rebuke the enemy is to fiercely deal with the bully of your soul.

James 4:7

> "Submit yourselves to God. Resist the devil and he will flee from you."

I love the Message translation of this verse:

> "So let God work his will in you. Yell a loud no to the Devil and watch him scamper." (The Message)

Rebuking is yelling a loud "No!!!" to the enemy and watching him scamper.

I had a crazy dream years ago that relates to this. I was having a bath, the tap was on and the bathtub was overflowing. All the water was spilling onto the bathroom floor and causing a huge mess. This was going to create some significant damage to our house.

In the midst of this crisis I called out to God, "Lord, turn off the tap!"

What do you think He said to me? That's right, He said...

"You turn it off!"

The dream ended.

I asked the Lord later that day what the dream meant. What I believe He showed me is that there are many things in my life I have the authority to address, but I ask Him to do it. He was inviting me to step into the authority He has given me in Jesus.

This is one of those situations. You must rebuke the enemy. Don't ask the Lord to deal with the demonic forces implementing the Whisper Campaign. You need to yell a loud "No!" to the enemy to let him know that you know he is a defeated foe. Let him know that you know you have all authority in heaven and on earth in Jesus' name. The enemy and his lies do not have authority over you. You have to stand up to the bully of your soul – command him to get out of your face.

This is not a prayer to the Lord - you are telling your enemy to go.

"Now I address the enemy of my soul in the name and authority of Jesus Christ – the risen Lord of Glory – and I command you to leave right now! I rebuke every lying spirit in the name of Jesus!!! You are not welcome and I say "No!!!!" to your lies. I rebuke Satan and every foul demonic spirit in the name of Jesus! Leave me alone. I bring the cross of Christ between me and your lies in the name of Jesus."

Again, be as specific as possible and name the particular lie, and its accompanying foul spirit that you want to leave. This is when the Spiritual Strangler Figs are being uprooted in your heart.

It may even be helpful to picture Spiritual Strangler Figs wrapped around your heart being miraculously uprooted by the power and authority of Jesus. Be fierce and rip those things up by the roots. Get rid of those lies, you don't want them around anymore.

Receive

Do you garden? My wife likes to garden a little, but she has a friend who is a voracious gardener. Her friend grows much of what she and her husband eat. Their garden is amazingly resplendent with all sorts of vegetables and fruits. They have had to do this because my wife's friend has some fairly significant health issues. She cannot allow herself to eat less than healthy food. All the food they grow is as natural as possible and because of their diligence to eat good, healthy foods her health is the best it has ever been.

Her garden is only resplendent because she is committed to 2 ongoing actions: 1. Plant and maintain healthy foods; 2. Pull out the weeds that would choke the life out of the healthy food.

The quality of her lifestyle is directly tied to the quality of food she eats.

You and I are no different. If we ingest the lies of the enemy on a regular basis we will live unhealthy, dark, oppressed, substandard lives far from the abundant life Jesus has for us. By walking through the first 3 Tools of Truth, you have pulled the spiritual weeds out of the garden of your heart. Now we need to make sure we plant and maintain Truth – the healthy foods we need to thrive and grow.

Plant and maintain the Truth, and pull out the lies. We must receive his Truth into our hearts.

What does that look like? There are 2 aspects to the Truth we need to receive: 1. The Rema Word of God – His spoken Word; 2. The Logos Word of God – His written Word.

We must practice listening prayer. Jesus speaks to us; we must learn to listen to Him and hear His heart toward us. Ask the Lord to reveal His heart for you. Ask for the Lord to heal your heart. God's heart is to heal you. He loves you. Receive His Truth. He wants to commune with you. He wants you to know His voice.

John 10:3-16

"...the sheep listen to his voice... The sheep follow him because they know his voice...they will never follow a stranger because they do not recognize a stranger's voice...the thief comes to steal, kill and destroy, I have come that they might have life and have it to the full...I am the good shepherd...I know my sheep and they know me...they listen to my voice."

Listening to and understanding the voice of God only happens by spending time alone with Him, communing with Him and His Word. "Devotions" are not a cute religious duty, they are critically important to appropriating the Truth of God in our lives.

We must intentionally plant the written word of God in our hearts. The only way we are going to get all the nutrients of the Truth of God's Word into our hearts is if we intentionally plant it there. That involves more than simply reading scripture. Sure reading is important. But if we are truly going to feed on Truth we need to move beyond reading to memorizing and meditating on God's Word.

Joshua 1:8

"Do not let this Book of the law depart from your mouth; mediate on it day and night, so that you may be careful to do everything written in it. Then you will be prosperous and successful."

To flourish in Jesus and experience the abundant life He has for us we must receive the Truth - intentionally plant it in our hearts through reading, memorizing and meditating on scripture.

To help you do this I have included a number of scriptures that have been significant in my life – ones I have committed to memory and regularly meditate on when the enemy comes at me with his Whisper Campaign:

Philippians 1:6

"I am confident of this very thing, that he who began a good work in you will be faithful to complete it."

Philippians 4:19

"My God will provide for all your needs according to His glorious riches in Christ Jesus."

Ephesians 3:20

"Now to Him who is able to do immeasurably more than what we can ask or imagine."

2 Corinthians 9:8

"And God is able to bless you abundantly, so that in all things at all times, having all that you need, you will abound in every good work."

Philippians 4:13

"I can do everything through him who gives me strength."

Romans 8:28

"And we know that in all things God works for the good of those who love him, who have been called according to his purpose."

Romans 8:31

"...if God is for us, who can be against us?!"

Romans 8:38-39

"...'nothing' will be able to separate us from the love of God that is in Christ Jesus our Lord."

Romans 8:15

"For you did not receive a spirit that makes you a slave again to fear, but you received the Spirit of sonship, and by Him we cry 'Abba Father'"

Psalm 32:8

"I will instruct you and teach you in the way you should go; I will counsel you and watch over you."

Psalm 27:13

"I am still confident of this; I will see the goodness of the Lord in the land of the living."

Psalm 9:9-10

"The Lord is a refuge for the oppressed, a stronghold in times of trouble. Those who know your name will trust in you, for you, Lord, have never forsaken those who seek you."

Philippians 2:13

"...for it is God who works in you to will and to act according to His good purpose."

2 Thessalonians 3:3

"But the Lord is faithful, and he will strengthen you and protect you from the evil one."

Colossians 1:13

"For He has rescued us from the dominion of darkness, and brought us into the kingdom of the Son he loves, in whom we have redemption, the forgiveness of sins."

Colossians 2:13-15

"When you were dead in your sins and in the uncircumcision of your flesh, God made you alive with Christ. He forgave us all our sins, having canceled the charge of our legal indebtedness, which stood against us and condemned us; he has taken it away, nailing it to the cross. And having disarmed the powers and authorities, he made a public spectacle of them, triumphing over them by the cross."

Jeremiah 29:11

"'For I know the plans I have for you' declares the Lord, 'plans to prosper you and not to harm you, plans to give you hope and a future. Then you will call upon me and come and pray to me, and I will listen to you. You will seek me and find me when you seek me with all your heart. I will be found by you', declares the Lord."

Jeremiah 31: 3

"I have loved you with an everlasting love; I have drawn you with loving-kindness."

Zephaniah 3:17

"The Lord your God is with you, he is mighty to save. He will take great delight in you, he will quiet you with his love, he will rejoice over you with singing."

I would like to suggest that you choose to take one of these scriptures each week and commit it to memory. Once you have memorized it, meditate on it as often as possible. Chew over each word in your mind – ask the Lord to help you to understand His Word and extract all the nutrients from it.

Have you ever watched a cow out in a field? It appears that the cow is continually chewing. Well, to a certain degree it is. The cow is not only eating and swallowing the grass, but it is also chewing its "cud". Cows are "ruminants" – animals with multi-chambered stomachs. In order to extract all the nutrients they can, ruminants chew and swallow grass then vomit it up and chew on "the cud". This enables them to extract more nutrients as they swallow it again into another chamber in their stomachs.

This is a picture of what we do when we meditate on scripture. When we memorize scripture we are swallowing it. When we bring it back again and chew on it some more we are meditating on it, thereby extracting more "spiritual nutrients".

You will experience greater and greater freedom the more you memorize and meditate on the Truth of scripture. The Truth will set you free! And freedom is a very good thing...

Rejoice

Do you have a happy dance?

My sister-in-law makes an amazing hummus. My brother is the Senior Pastor of a church in Winnipeg, Manitoba with a large number of immigrants in the congregation. Many people wanting to start a new life in Canada land in Winnipeg, and my brother's church reaches out to care for these people who come from many different nations. One of the ways they do this is to host them in their home for an after church meeting lunch. My sister-in-law is a master of hospitality providing sumptuous meals in a wonderfully welcoming and loving environment.

She has one secret weapon – her hummus. It is utterly amazing. She told me of an occasion when they had some international guests over, one of whom was from Latin America. When he tasted her hummus he started to dance.

"What are you doing?" she asked.

He replied, "This is my happy dance! This is the most amazing hummus I have ever tasted!"

This guy knew how to rejoice about life's simple pleasures. He chose to rejoice over some great hummus.

How much more do we have to rejoice in knowing we have been set free from the bullying, oppression and lies of the enemy! Unfortunately though, Jesus followers can sometimes act like we have been baptised in bad vinegar – not much joy.

We need to learn to choose to rejoice in God's goodness, grace, freedom and Truth. This is a time for joyful thanksgiving - we have been set free from the bondage of the lies of the enemy. Be thankful for the victory the Lord has given you. Be thankful for the life He has promised you. Your chains are gone. You don't need to be bullied anymore. You have overcome. You have the victory. Whom the Lord has set free is free indeed!!!!

Philippians 4:4

"Rejoice in the Lord always! I will say it again – rejoice!"

Romans 14:17

"For the kingdom of God is not a matter of eating and drinking, but of righteousness, peace and joy in the Holy Spirit"

Nehemiah 8:10

"...Do not grieve, for the joy of the LORD is your strength."

Rejoicing is a choice.

There is a Scottish Proverb that says, "Never give a sword to a man who can't dance."

What I believe this means is we cannot love battle, we can't love war because it's life we are fighting for. It's about the life of the Kingdom of God in us and through us. It's about the dance, not the fight.

It's not about the battle. Sure we have to fight through spiritual opposition to appropriate the life Jesus has for us, but we fight so we can have the life. We fight so we can dance.

If you want to see a simple yet profound expression of rejoicing watch professional sports games. Watch the crowd when their team scores. What happens? People cheer, they shout, they embrace, they jump up and down, they raise their hands, they sing and they dance. And, that is a choice. They could choose to sit down and do a little clap or a quiet "woohoo", or they can choose to let loose and rejoice.

To rejoice is a choice. Scripture is pretty clear: we must choose to rejoice. We certainly have lots to celebrate! What have you got to lose except your own self-consciousness? And if you really take a deep look into your "self" consciousness, you will discover it is rooted in a lie of the enemy – it's called the "fear of man". That simply means you are more concerned about what people think of you than what God thinks of you.

45

Rip that Spiritual Strangler Fig out and get free!

I am a child of the 70's so some of the nostalgic music that takes me back to great memories of my youth is disco. Now, don't judge me, I like all kinds of music, but there are some disco songs that are awesome. I particularly like a couple of Earth Wind and Fire Songs. These guys weren't Jesus followers, but they understood the Truth about choosing to rejoice.

My favourite song of theirs is "Sing a Song". The essence of the song is similar to that expressed by King David in many psalms. The lyrics encourage listeners to sing a song to make your day better. Sing a song to make a better way.

Are you feeling down and out? Sing a song! Do you find yourself caught in despair and you're downcast? Sing a song! It's tough to smile? Sing a song!

Choose to believe. Declare the Truth. Give yourself what you need – feed on the Truth and believe it. Don't retreat. Move forward in the Truth.

"Bless the Lord O my soul!" "I will see the goodness of God in the land of the living!" "God is an ever present help in times of trouble!" "God has never yet forsaken any who put their trust in Him!" "The Lord reigns, let the earth rejoice!"

Let's choose to rejoice in God's great goodness and His good greatness. Sing His praises. Sing of His great goodness and His good greatness. Sing of His love. Sing of our freedom in Him. Sing of His victory over the enemy of our souls. Sing the Truth. Sing a song!

Wholeheartedly worship Him. It's not about you - it's about Him. Lose your self-consciousness in the ocean of God-consciousness. Get over yourself. We have so much to celebrate. The joy of the Lord is definitely our strength.

Do you want to know something that will totally change your life?

OK, lean in, let me whisper this to you – the Truth of it will change you if you really get hold of it.

Do you know what the joy of the Lord is?

You.

Yup, you are the joy of the Lord.

Hebrews 12:1-2

"Therefore, since we are surrounded by such a great cloud of witnesses, let us throw off everything that hinders us and the sin that so easily entangles, and let us run with perseverance the race marked out for us. Let us fix our eyes on Jesus, the author and perfecter of our faith, who for the joy set before Him endured the cross, scorning its shame, and sat down at the right hand of the throne of God."

The joy set before Jesus is you and me – God's beloved sons and daughters set free from the enemy. No more being bullied by the enemy of our soul. The chains of sin and death have been broken and we can live in the abundant life Jesus purchased for us. God's Kingdom has come, His life and His will being done in and through the lives of His children. On earth as it is in heaven. There is a new sheriff in town. We don't need to be pushed around by the bad guys anymore!

Scripture tells us that the Lord delights in us so much He rejoices over us with singing:

Zephaniah 3:17

"The Lord your God is with you, he is mighty to save. He will take great delight in you, he will quiet you with his love, he will rejoice over you with singing."

God's heart toward you is delight, not disappointment. That is worth celebrating. That is worth rejoicing, and so much more.

I want to encourage you to do something: ask God to help you hear a song He sings over you...

I was driving to meet an out-of-town client one brilliantly sunny September day. I had the top down in my convertible Jeep as I wove through the mountains with a caramel macchiato in hand and the latest James Taylor CD beginning to play.

What an awesome day! Sunshine, convertible, mountain drive, caramel macchiato and James Taylor – a perfect day! I was really looking forward to sharing this drive with Jesus. As one particular song began to play, I started to get emotional. Tears began to well up in my eyes.

Now for me, when emotion begins to well up I know the Holy Spirit is up to something. So I asked the Lord what He was up to. I sensed Him whisper this to me,

"I am singing this song over you…"

As I listened to the James Taylor song "It's Growing", these were the words I heard,

"My love for you grows and it grows. Whoa, whoa, whoa how it grows and grows. And where it's gonna stop nobody knows. Hey, hey, hey, nobody knows."

It was a song of love my Heavenly Father was singing over me. I drank it in and let it touch the depth of my soul. He was rejoicing over me with singing.

Your Heavenly Father rejoices over you with singing too! Your Daddy delights in you. Ask the Lord to help you hear a song He is singing over you, and then drink it in.

IT'S TIME TO FIGHT

George McFly wasn't what you would call bold and courageous. In fact, he wasn't even close to that. To describe him would be to use words like timid, fearful, insecure, mousy – a wimp. He was constantly bullied by Biff, the big intimidating, dominating, bombastic bane of George's life.

What was the cure for George? Well, his son Marty went back in time to change things up a bit. In the movie Back to the Future Marty sets out to change his dad by orchestrating an event that would enable him to win the heart of his future wife and man-up in the process.

One problem though: Marty's future mom had inadvertently fallen for Marty, her future son, and not George, her future husband. Marty had messed things up in a way that would change the future and eliminate his existence. He had to right the wrong he had created.

So, he hatched a plan with George. Marty would pretend to take advantage of his future mom in the car outside the prom. George would discover them and come to her rescue by beating up Marty, thereby winning her heart and asserting his masculine strength and building his confidence.

Simple, right?

Wrong. Another problem occurred: somehow Marty didn't get to the car and Biff ended up accosting George's future wife in the car. She starts really screaming for help. George walks up ready to enact the plan by swinging open the door to tell Marty to stop or else.

The problem is, when he swings open the door to put the plan in place he discovers his arch nemesis Biff, not Marty. He is tempted to walk away knowing he cannot overcome Biff. However, he cannot not step in to help the girl whose heart he wants to win. So, against the tide of fear overwhelming him he tells Biff to stop.

Biff gets out of the car and lets George know he is about to get the beating of his life. George tries to punch him, but Biff easily grabs his feeble punch and begins to twist his arm to the point of breaking, driving George into submission.

The love of George's life hops out of the car to jump on Biff's back telling him to let George go. He pushes her crashing onto the ground with one hand and shifts his attention from George to laugh at her humiliating state sprawled on the ground.

This is where things begin to change. Deep down, deep in the recesses of his heart a fire is ignited in George. The pain and frustration from the years of bullying, humiliation, taunting, oppression, and settling for less than real life begins to turn into anger and violence in George. He steps into his courage and strength to deliver a knockout blow to Biff.

Like the old Kenny Rogers song "Coward of the County", George "...let him have it all." Biff ends up unconscious on the ground. His damsel in distress is smitten, love blooms, strength, confidence and freedom reigns in George, and of course, they live happily ever after.

My point is this, if George McFly can do it, you can. If George can stand up to the bully so can you. Your spiritual bully has been defeated by Jesus and you have the authority of Christ in Jesus' name. The enemy knows that, he simply wants to know if you know that.

Let him know with both barrels! Let him have it all!

James 4:7

> "Submit yourselves, then, to God. Resist the devil, and he will flee from you."

> "So let God work his will in you. Yell a loud no to the Devil and watch him scamper." (The Message)

Years ago I saw a Canadian Armed Forces recruiting brochure. On the front was a lone soldier standing in an open field with the caption, "You stand alone." When you opened it up the photo revealed a broader perspective on the lone soldier. You could now see he was surrounded by massive amounts of fire power: tanks, artillery, fighter jets, and much, much more.

The caption read, "But you are never alone."

The reality is, you stand alone too, but you are never alone. You have the Spirit of the Living God alive in you. You have all authority in the name of Jesus. You are fighting a defeated foe, who contests his defeat to find out if you know the Truth and are committed to appropriating it. In addition, you are surrounded by a great cloud of witnesses cheering you on.

And, God commands His angels concerning you. The truth is, there are myriad angels ready to engage with you in your fight against the demonic oppression set against you. The war in the spirit realm is very real, and your decision to step in in the name of Jesus in His authority drastically changes the outcome. The hosts of heaven, the angels of God step in and fight on your behalf.

Psalm 91:11

"For he will command his angels concerning you to guard you in all your ways."

You are definitely not alone.

At the Canadian Military Museum at Juno beach in Normandy there is a very moving landing craft display. You actually get into a landing craft and make the simulated journey to the beaches of Normandy to commence the battle for the freedom of Europe on D-Day.

While you stand in the landing craft you are surrounded by the sights and sounds with which the men on June 6, 1941 were surrounded. As I was intently engaging in this experience I heard the prayer of a man in the audio of the simulation. His prayer caught my attention, landing deep in my heart,

"God help me because this is about more than just me."

You getting free from the lies of the enemy is not just about your own liberation. You now become an ambassador of Truth so God's Kingdom can come and His will can be done in you and through you to others. No, this is not just about you. Your freedom is the beginning of so much more.

The jig is up. The strategy of the enemy has been exposed. We understand the Whisper Campaign and the Spiritual Strangler Fig. It's time to surrender and fight, and believe the Truth of God not the lies of the enemy.

The hosts of Heaven are ready. The great cloud of witnesses is cheering you on. The Spirit of the Living God is alive in you. Jesus has overcome your enemies. Your heavenly Father delights in you, and God has a whole new way for you to live known as the epic adventure of the Kingdom of God.

Your freedom and life is worth your effort. And even more so, the freedom and life of others through you is worth your effort. There is so much more in God's heart for us and through us.

Let's take Him at His Word and jump in with both feet, and both barrels.

1 Corinthians 2:9

> "No eye has seen, no ear has heard, no mind has conceived what God has prepared for those who live Him."

Ephesians 3:20

> "Now to Him who is able to do immeasurably more than all we ask or imagine, according to his power that is at work within us."

ABOUT THE AUTHOR

Dave MacLean is a speaker, writer, entrepreneur, husband, father, brother, son and friend. He has spent his career in the marketplace as a "marketplace minister". He believes that full time ministry is an attitude, not a position, and, therefore, sees his work in the business community as ministry.

Through the work of Wholehearted Men Dave envisions and equips men to live wholeheartedly in Jesus. Dave's desire is to partner with God to facilitate His breath of life breathing on the dry bones of men's lives, as depicted in Ezekiel 37. Dave delivers one day conferences and weekend "boot camps" for men and couples. He has written numerous books and study guides, and also writes a weekly e-visional called "How's The Viz?".

More information can be found at
www.wholeheartedmen.com

Through the work of Wholehearted Leaders Dave works with marketplace leaders to envision and equip them to live and lead "wholeheartedly" – from a deep sense of identity, conviction, commitment, passion, purpose and life. Dave's desire is to empower socially conscious leaders to lead and live on purpose, from the heart. Dave writes a weekly newspaper column and blog for leaders called "ENCOURAGEMENTS".

More information can be found at
www.wholeheartedleaders.com